WHAT TEENS ARE SAYING ABOUT MICHELLE A. HANSEN!

I liked learning about how to cope with stress — how it can affect you mentally and physically. *(Karyme, age 15)*

The most important thing I learned was that I am in control of my own happiness and emotions. It's important because I don't have to be miserable. *(Marissa, age 16)*

I learned to always follow my dreams. It's important to me because I like to dream big, and knowing if I can accomplish enough I can get to it. *(Melinna, age 16)*

The most important thing is when we talked about friendship. Because I really need help on that. *(Fatima, age 11)*

You will get a lot of helpful tips that you will need in the future. *(Bailey, age 16)*

You see things in different perspectives and learn things that can and will make your life so much easier. *(Emilee, age 14)*

I thought I would HATE this workshop but I legitimately cried when it ended. I had SUCH a great time. It didn't even feel awkward AT ALL!! *(Kasi, age 12)*

Thank you for giving me reminders that I can control my day and my happiness. All of your talks were really interesting and I really enjoyed them. *(Elizabeth, age 14)*

Want to get the most from this book? Scan the QR code at the beginning of each chapter and watch Michelle's video introduction for that chapter.

New to QR codes? No problem. Go to www.michelleahansen.com/videos for a quick tutorial on how to download and use a QR reader to make your reading experience more fun.

Relax, girl!
YOU GOT THIS

CONNECT WITH MICHELLE A. HANSEN!

Join a community of dreamers, leaders, goal-setters and change-makers. Girls Change the World is a community for girls like you. Learn all about it here:

Still not using a QR code reader? Why not? Okay, try this: www.michelleahansen.com/joinme

Relax, girl!
YOU GOT THIS

Your Guide to a Fun and Stress-Free High School Experience

BY MICHELLE A. HANSEN

Priest Rapids Press
Mattawa, WA
2017

Relax, Girl! You Got This
Michelle A. Hansen

Published by Priest Rapids Press
Mattawa, WA

ISBN-13: 978-0-9994629-0-4
ISBN-10: 0-9994629-0-3

Manufactured in the United States of America
10 9 8 7 6 5 4 3 2 1

For Mazie and Josie —
You bless the world every day.

WHO IS MICHELLE A. HANSEN?
WHY SHOULD YOU LISTEN TO HER ANYWAY?

In 2001, Michelle A. Hansen and her class of high school students were held hostage by a teen gunman. This experience transformed Michelle from an average teacher into a passionate advocate for teens, a committed mentor, author, and empowerment coach.

Michelle is on a mission to help teens step into their highest potential without stressing themselves out. As a recovering over-achiever, she knows firsthand how easy it is to fall into the "never enough" trap.

Michelle was the daughter of a county undersheriff who taught her to shoot a pistol and drive when she was eleven years old. She grew up on a farm in southeastern Washington state, where she loved horses a whole lot more than books. Thanks to an inspired English teacher, Michelle fell in love with reading in the seventh grade. She earned a Bachelor of Arts in English Teaching from Brigham Young University and a Master of Fine Arts in Creative Writing from the Northwest Institute of Literary Arts. She is the author of two young adult novels: *Before They Find Us* (2013) and *Painted Blind* (2012). She and her husband reside in Washington state with their four children. Connect with Michelle at www.michelleahansen.com.

TABLE OF CONTENTS

HEY THERE, FRESHMAN.

Imagine this. Your bags are packed. Your best hiking shoes are on your feet. You are ready to begin the journey that will take you from where you are right now to the best, brightest, happiest version of yourself.

Are you ready? Today is your day.

It's your day to shine. It's your day to throw off the baggage that has kept you stuck. It's your day to reinvent yourself into the "you" you've always dreamed of being.

This journey is a wild ride. It's exhilarating and fun, and sometimes it's terrifying. Never fear. You don't walk alone. You have friends, family and teachers to support you, to pull you up when you fall, to lead you out of the dark, and to help you see the road signs that are blocked by your life's fog. You've got me to teach you new strategies and tricks that will open previously unimaginable possibilities. You will find other mentors along the way, too.

Most importantly, today you take the first step. Tomorrow you take another. Baby steps can take you all the way up Mt. Everest, but you have to keep moving to get to the top.

Are you ready to get started? Awesome. Let's do this.

Chapter 1
FRESHMAN YEAR

Here it is! Your freshman year. You've finally made it to high school. Before you are four years that will help define you and your future. While this transition into high school is fun and exciting, it can also be downright scary.

Almost as soon as Morgan[1] stepped out the doors of her middle school in June, she began stressing about high school. Would the upper classmen pick on her? Would she be able to keep up with her classes? Would she make the volleyball team or be humiliated by being cut after working so hard in middle school? Before she'd experienced a single day of high school, Morgan's imagination had run wild with worst-case scenarios until she'd decided that high school would suck, she'd be miserable, and maybe she should just home school.

Can you relate?

High school does bring changes. Usually two or three middle schools feed into one high school.

---

[1] All names have been changes to protect privacy.

New faces and a schedule full of new classes often cause a natural shift in friend groups. You may be afraid of losing the closeness you have with your current friends. You may also fear that once the friend shuffle is over, you'll be left standing alone. Friend groups in high school also become more dependent on common sports and activities.

> "Freedom lies in being bold."
>
> Robert Frost

High school sports and activities are more competitive and more time consuming. Everything from football to drama to band to cheer demands a year-round commitment. Students feel increased individual pressure to rise to higher standards of performance, so the team will excel. Some teens thrive on this competition, while others feel crushed by it and fall by the wayside. If you stay in, you have less and less time for your other friends, less to talk about, fewer shared experiences until you begin to drift apart.

Harder classes also worry many freshmen. Teachers expect more time spent on homework at the same time coaches and advisors are requiring more hours at practice and competitions. Now your grades are recorded on transcripts you'll be sending to colleges. You're pulled into meetings with counselors and parents, planning out classes and career paths and credits. Before you even begin classes, you feel the pressure that suddenly things matter more than they did before.

Finally, there's the dating scene. Many freshmen

feel increased pressure to be in a romantic relationship. Once in a relationship, there is added pressure to engage in sexual activity, even if you don't feel ready. This pressure can be magnified when you date upperclassmen.

All of these changes understandably cause you to feel apprehensive about this new phase of your life. However, let me assure you, you are going to thrive. Sure, you'll have ups and downs. You'll make friends and lose some. You'll ace tests, and you'll probably fail some. It's okay. It's part of the learning process.

You'll do fun, exciting things and boring, stupid things over the next four years, but the most important thing for you to know is that these years are *yours*. They belong to you, not your parents, not your teachers, not your coaches. These are *your* years to forge an authentic identity and lay the foundation for a life you'll love living.

So many demands will be placed on you over the next four years—assignments to complete, expectations to meet, rules to follow, grades to earn—what *you want* can easily get lost in the shuffle.

Did you know that stress is the number one emotion teens report feeling on a regular basis? Not joy, not happiness. Stress, with a capital S.

Eighty-three percent of teens report that school is the number one cause of their stress[i] and sleep deprivation among teens is practically an epidemic.

Why does this matter?

Prolonged stress can be devastating to your health, leading to headaches, back pain, anxiety, fatigue, weight gain, diabetes, and heart problems.[ii]

According to Dr. Fred Luskin, "Stress leads us to make poor choices that limit our ability to deal with the challenges in our lives."[iii]

Let me be honest here. As a demographic, teens aren't known for the best decision-making skills. Prolonged stress can be the difference between, "Oops. That was stupid. Remind me not to do that again," and "Oh, shizzle! My parents are going to *KILL* me!"

You know what I'm saying?

Now imagine your graduation day. You're decked out in your cap and gown, school-colored tassel hanging in your eyes. You think back on the last four years.

How do you want to feel in that moment?

Do you want to celebrate with no regrets, knowing you lived true to your vision for yourself and had meaningful connections along the way? Or, do you want to look back on a blur of stress, anxiety, and missed opportunities, trading the hamster wheel of high school for a bigger hamster wheel in college? Your approach to high school, your ability to cope with stress, and your intentional decision to cultivate an authentic self will make all the difference between those two scenarios.

I'm here to give you simple steps to make high school stress-free and fun.

EXERCISE:

Before we begin, record how you're feeling right now about going to high school.

Scan this code to see
the video introduction.

Chapter 2
THE FEAR MONSTER

In the previous chapter, we talked about some natural shifts that come with the move from middle school to high school. We acknowledged that these shifts may cause fear. So, let's talk about fear for a moment.

Imagine you really want to sing in a talent show. You've never performed alone on stage. You're afraid. How do you handle that fear?

Do you pretend the fear doesn't exist and go on stage anyway? Or do you decide you're not ready to perform on stage? Maybe next year.

If you chose A, you might consider yourself courageous. If you chose B, you might feel like a coward. As a culture, we are not good at dealing with fear. Most people tend to ignore their fear and put on a brave act, or they give into fear and beat themselves up over it.

What is fear anyway?
Fear is simply a warning system. It is your

body's natural way of telling you that something potentially dangerous is in your near future. Fear is intended to keep you safe. If you come face to face with a hungry bear, fear keeps you from walking up and trying to pet its nose. Fear triggers several biological functions to help you survive. Your heart beats faster. Your breathing gets shallow and quick. Your visual focus narrows on the danger and blocks out other distractions. Your body releases adrenaline which helps you react quickly with more strength.

Once you're out of danger, the body relaxes. Your systems that were in overdrive dip below normal as compensation for their previous elevated state before leveling off to normal. Fear has done its job keeping you alive.

The problem is that most of your fears today are not keeping you from life-threatening danger. Often fear is keeping you from living fully and freely. Your subconscious brain likes what it knows. The brain's natural response to anything unfamiliar is fear. Whenever you try to do something you've never done, you can expect a fear response of some degree. The brain confuses "new" for "dangerous."

Ignoring fear and pretending to be brave may *seem* like a good, courageous response, but it can backfire. Fear is a product of your subconscious brain. That subconscious will keep hounding you until you listen and acknowledge it. What I'm saying is that fear ignored means fear multiplied until you move the experience into the realm of the familiar.

If you simply pretend you're not afraid, your

subconscious doesn't like it. When it realizes its warnings are being ignored, the subconscious sends bigger warnings. Pretending you're not afraid actually allows your fear to grow. Being afraid doesn't make you weak. Remember that fear is a product of the subconscious brain. It is not rational like your conscious brain. You really cannot control how fear appears, only what you do with it once it pops up.

> *"Courage is not the absence of fear, but rather the judgment that something else is more important than fear."*
>
> *Ambrose Redmoon*

It's impossible to live completely free of fear because fear will show up in some degree every time you try something new and unfamiliar. So, how do you accept fear without becoming crippled by it?

When my son first got his driver's license, I had a terrible nightmare in which he died in a car accident. I started awake, terrified and crying. The fear of losing him was crippling. I wanted to shove that fear away and never feel it again, but I knew that fear ignored is fear that grows. I lay there in bed and moved into the fear. I allowed myself to experience it fully. I allowed myself to taste for a moment the devastation I'd feel if that nightmare became my reality. Then, at the height of this fear, I told myself, "If this happened, it would be horrible, but it has not happened. If it does happen, I will deal with it. Right now I am going to cherish every day with my son."

Within a few minutes, the fear evaporated, and I

was able to sleep again.

You can use the same strategy to release your fears, whether they concern school, friends, family, or another issue. Let me give you three simple steps: acknowledge it, feel it, and release it.

Acknowledge, Feel, Release

First, acknowledge the fear. Acknowledging fear doesn't mean you let it control you. Instead it means you recognize its existence. You allow it to have a voice. That voice doesn't control your actions, but the voice gets heard. Let's go back to the example of singing in the talent show. All day before the show, you're jittery and nervous. Ignoring your fear would mean you pretend you're not nervous. You're fine. You do nothing to deal with those nerves. Acknowledging fear is a mental process in which you simply say, "What am I afraid of?" Then answer that question:

I'm afraid I won't be able to hit the high notes.

I'm afraid people will laugh at me.

I'm afraid I'll forget the words.

Now instead of pushing the fear away, you move into it. You allow yourself to fully feel the fear, giving your subconscious a voice. You're feeling the exact thing your subconscious wants you to avoid. Yes, you'd be horrified if you couldn't hit the high notes. Yes, you'd feel humiliated if people laughed at you. Yes, you'd feel silly if you forgot the words. You *feel* what the fear is trying to tell you.

Next, retake control of your emotion. Now that your subconscious has spoken to you through fear, tell it clearly, "That has not happened. If it happens, I will deal with it. I will survive it, but until then, I am going to go forward with a positive attitude." Now that you've taken control, you can allow the fear to release. Yes, you would feel bad if people laughed, but that has not happened. It's not going to happen because you've practiced this song a gazillion times. You can sing it perfectly.

You chose to go forward anyway. Basically, you're telling fear, "Thank you for your input. Now I'm going to do whatever I want." Your turn in the talent show arrives. You have butterflies flopping around your stomach, but you decide that you are going to do this, even though you're nervous. You sing your number, and perfect or not, you receive wild applause. The fear response releases. Your brain takes in this positive feedback. The experience of singing on stage has now moved from unfamiliar and scary to familiar with positive feedback. You acted in the presence of fear, and you won. Next time you try to sing on stage, this positive experience will be part of your conscious and subconscious experience. That's not to say that you won't be nervous, but you'll probably be less nervous than you were the first time.

Some fears are deeply rooted in your subconscious. You may have to release them again and again. That's okay. Just keep doing this process until the fear loses its power.

A Final Thought on Fear
People who accomplish great things do not do it in the absence of fear. They do it with fear as a

silent companion. They understand how to acknowledge their fear, feel it, and act anyway.

So, here you are on the threshold of high school. Like Morgan you may have many strong fears pushing at your mind, or you may have subtle fears that you've been trying to ignore. Either way, take a moment to acknowledge those fears. Remember, fear is irrational. It doesn't have to make sense to exist.

"You gain strength, courage, and confidence by every experience in which you really stop to look fear in the face." Eleanor Roosevelt

---

EXERCISE:
1. Think about going to high school. What concerns big and small do you have about the next four years? Take a moment and write them down. Write your big fears and your small, silly fears.
2. Practice the 3-step fear releasing strategy on your biggest fear. Repeat it each day for a week, and record your progress.

Scan this code to see
the video introduction.

Chapter 3
A VISION OF YOU

At some time during elementary school you were probably introduced to goal setting. It's a simple concept. You pick something you want to accomplish. You write out steps that will get you there. Then you vow to work *really* hard until you achieve your goal.

The problem with simple goal-setting is that you have to rely on willpower and determination to accomplish your goals. Inadvertently, you focus on the work not the reward. You do things the way you've always done them, you just try harder to do more.

Eventually your familiar patterns and habits pull you back to where you were before you set the goal, and maybe you decide you didn't want that goal all that much anyway. Without enough motivation to keep moving forward, most people fall off the wagon in a matter of days. Just ask anyone who's ever made a new year's resolution to exercise or lose weight. Very few people make lasting change.

When you set a goal and you fail to reach it, the pain of failing is worse than the pain you felt before you set the goal in the first place. Your motivation to change falls even farther. You feel stuck. Why bother? Maybe you convince yourself it's hopeless. You'll never change.

Does this sound like fun? No wonder only a fraction of the population regularly sets goals.

> *"Be brave enough to live the life of your dreams according to your vision and purpose instead of the expectations and opinions of others."*
>
> *Roy T. Bennett*

Vision is different. Vision doesn't seek to change you. It seeks to change your results by tapping into the most authentic version of yourself. Your authentic self is perfect and whole. It's unchangeable because it's rooted in a divine connection to the Universe. Your authentic self is the very best you that is waiting to emerge. It's the you that is hiding beneath the ego, the pride, the resentments, and the fear. True vision allows you to free your most authentic self and learn to become that self.

Visioning is the North Star of goal setting. When you create vision, you create a complete picture of what you want to be, do, and have. Vision is deeply connected to your unique personality, your life mission, and your individual path to joy. You're not just creating a vision of stuff you want to own or places you want to see. You're creating a vision of the person you want to be as you venture into adulthood.

Think of your life as being supported by four key pillars:

- Health and wellness
- Relationships
- Academics and future career
- Free time and personal development

Your ideal vision creates a picture of what your life would be like if, on a scale of one to ten, every aspect of your life was a ten plus, plus, plus.

Create the Vision

Think about the perfect life that you want to create. You have four years of high school and four to eight years of college to get on the path to that life. Many of the things you want out of life are not somewhere out there in the future. They are right here, right now, and you can have them while you're building your future dreams. What are the things you want to *do*? Who do you want to *know*? What do you want to *learn*? How do you want to *feel*?

Your big dreams have a feeling tone. Imagine yourself living the life you dream of. How does that feel when you wake up every morning? Wouldn't you jump out of bed and think, "I love my life!" Even when your life isn't perfect, you can create the same feeling tone. If you jumped out of bed every morning with that exuberant, happy feeling, and thought, "I love my life!" pretty soon, you would be living a life you love, because your state of being will attract like physical circumstances into your life.

So, what do you want to do over the next four years that will get you excited about life? Do you want to run cross country? Be on the dance team? Get elected to an ASB office? Do you want to make friends with a senior who can help you navigate the social scene? Do you want to learn how to edit video or be a social media influencer? Most importantly, how do you want to feel? Do you want to live each day with confidence? Do you want to feel a sense of purpose as you volunteer for a great cause? If each aspect of your life was *A-MAZ-ING*, what would that feel like? Allow yourself to feel it while you create the vision.

Remember, everyone's vision is different because what makes you happy is completely individual.

Now, you might be asking, "Why create a vision at all? Why not wing it?"

"Winging it" is how most people live their lives. They don't really have a clear picture of what they want and where they are going, and to paraphrase the Cheshire Cat in *Alice in Wonderland*, if you don't know where you're going, any road will take you there. The problem is that most people don't end up where they want to be, then they blame God, their parents and the government because they are not happy. They didn't get what they really wanted because they never clearly defined what they wanted and they never got on the path to getting it.

If you want to end up in a place that will bring you happiness, a place that fits who you are and how you want to live, creating a vision is the simplest, most straightforward way to get started on your way to that life.

The Trap of False Vision

Now, I have to warn you, creating an authentic vision can be tricky. I'll explain why. Let's say you envisioned yourself as the most popular girl in school. Your life mission for the next four years is to be popular. Stop and ask yourself why. Why do I want that? Is it because I want the validation of knowing people like me? Is it because I want the status of being able to do whatever I want without people making fun of me? Is it because my sister was Homecoming Queen, and I want to measure up? Is it because I want to have dozens of friends?

This is a false vision. This is your ego seeking external validation. That's not what visions are made of. Being popular isn't inherently bad, but why you want it matters. It matters a lot. If you want it to feed your pride and puff up your ego, that is a false vision and will not create lasting happiness.

Visions are the product of your uniqueness seeking to emerge. Vision doesn't need external validation because true vision makes you feel alive. That full-of-life, expansive feeling alone makes a vision worth pursuing.

A completely self-serving vision will not bring you lasting joy. It will be hollow from day one, and no amount of success will make it otherwise.

Real vision gives you the life you want *and* has a positive impact on others.

Most people think they want an honor (like being voted to Homecoming court) or a thing (like a Ferrari) when actually, they want a feeling they think it will bring them. Your ego creates a false vision in order to express the feelings you lack. It tells you that if you drive a Ferrari, you'll feel confident and happy. You will feel respected and admired. Guess what? Feeling confident, happy, even respected and admired all happen on the inside. Happiness is an inside job, so is confidence. Respect and admiration don't come to people because they drive Ferraris. Respect and admiration come because of who people became and what they accomplished in order to buy a Ferrari. That, really, is what most people want.

> *"The only thing worse than being blind is having sight and no vision."*
>
> *Helen Keller*

Here is the most priceless life lesson I've learned. I'm passing it onto you, free of charge. Are you ready?

Listen carefully.

The thing doesn't bring you the feeling. The feeling attracts the thing you desire.

Being voted to the Homecoming court won't automatically give you dozens of friends, but taking a sincere interest in the people around you, being genuine and kind to them, and looking out for them *will* win you dozens of friends. That is what you really want, and you control that outcome completely. You can decide that you will be confident, happy, and cultivate genuine friendships today.

Now consider someone who wants popularity at all costs. You can see right through that. You know when you're being used. You know when someone is pretending to like you for the sake of a vote. That person doesn't have dozens of real friends. Instead, she weaves a web of falsehood, insincerity, and insecurity in an effort to buy a feeling tone that is missing on the inside.

> "Only vision allows us to transform dreams of greatness into the reality of achievement through human action. Vision has no boundaries and knows no limits.
>
> Our vision is what we become in life."
>
> Tony Dungy

Don't let your ego deceive you into believing that other people dictate how you feel. The most important friend you have is the one looking back at you in the mirror. You tell that friend how to feel, and no one else can change that unless you let them. Remember that true vision is a product of your divine self, which has unique gifts to develop and share with the world. Real vision will always have some good in it for others because you're not here on this earth to collect possessions. You're here to do amazing things that will benefit yourself and the people around you.

There are two essential questions that will help you determine if this vision is worth your life's energy. First, is there good in it for others? Second, is this vision worth your time?

Your time on earth is unrepeatable. Time is the only limited commodity in life. Will your vision pay dividends of authentic joy and happiness? Will you be a better person for having obtained this vision? If so, you are on the right track.

Capture the Vision

Now it's time to capture your ideal vision. In your imagination walk through a perfect day. See yourself getting A's on all your assignments and tests. See yourself chatting with friends who value and appreciate you. See yourself fulfilling the duties of the activities in which you want to be involved. Imagine yourself completing a project with your newly-learned skills. See yourself opening an acceptance letter from the college of your choice.

Get inside this vision. Try not to see yourself from the outside, but see the vision as if you are living it right now. If you want to be on the dance team, imagine standing on the gym floor looking up at the crowd. Imagine how your dance uniform feels on your body. Imagine the beat of the music thumping in your ears.

Here is the number one, most important thing about your vision: it should excite you.

If you imagine yourself being, doing, and having all the things you want, and that vision doesn't exhilarate you, it's not your true vision.

It's more likely a product of your ego or of social pressure. On the first pass most of us create a vision of what we think we should want instead of what we actually want as a unique and independent human being.

It may take some time and thought to uncover your true vision. After all, you've spent years being influenced by your friends, family, and the media. Their expectations often cloud true vision, but once you set your mind to uncovering your vision, you will find it.

Some people are reluctant to create a vision because they are afraid to be stuck with a single image of their future. Don't worry. Your vision will grow and evolve with you. What's important now is to create a vision that excites you. You aren't stuck with it forever, but it will get you moving along the path to your dreams.

Now that you've experienced the vision in your imagination, and you've felt the excitement of it, it's time to capture that vision in writing. Writing down the vision solidifies its existence. Instead of a passing fantasy that will be forgotten tomorrow, this vision will remain, and you'll be able to come back to it again and again.

Spend some time creating a vision for your next four years of high school and beyond. Specifically, imagine and record what you want to do, who you want to know, what you want to learn, and how you want to feel. As you read over your vision, allow it to create a sense of excitement inside you. If it doesn't excite you, keep revising until you have a vision that you'll love living.

Scan this code to see the video introduction.

Chapter 4
THE GIFT YOU GIVE YOURSELF

There is a coveted attribute that most people desire. You may have some, very little, or a lot of this attribute, but one thing is certain. Most people want more.

I'm talking about confidence.

Often teens have the erroneous belief that confidence is a product of accomplishments and the feedback you receive from others. This is simply not true.

They say it takes ten positive comments to outweigh one negative comment. We live in an overly negative world. If you're relying on outside feedback to love yourself, you're always going to be in the red.

Real confidence comes from within. Confidence comes from knowing who you are, honoring that self, and living in a way that allows that self to grow and develop its full potential. No one can give that to you. No amount of compliments can create it in you. Confidence is not the result of accomplishments. Actually, the opposite is true. Most people's accomplishments come as a result of their confidence and their willingness to take risks. Without confidence, people play small. They let opportunities pass by because they are afraid of failing or making a fool out of themselves.

Especially now as you transition into high school, your confidence will be tested. You are in the process of developing your identity. You may have had a great experience in middle school, or it may have been a living hell. For some of you, you're looking forward to high school as a fresh start and a much needed break from the old cliques. For others, high school threatens to tear apart your comfortable bubble.

Either way, your confidence is probably going to need some love, now and throughout the school year.

Make the Choice

Your teen years are a confusing time because you're trying to figure out where you fit in this world. You're trying to discover your strengths and overcome your weaknesses. You're being pushed through academic hoops that sometimes exhaust and belittle your confidence.

If there was *one thing* I wish I could go back and teach my teenage self, it is this: *Your identity doesn't come from outside you.*

Too many teens are waiting for their peers or their parents or their teachers to tell them who they should be. They're waiting for someone to give them permission to become something great. It doesn't work that way. You're already something great. You just haven't nurtured that greatness.

Other people cannot define you because they don't really know you. They only know what you show them. Therefore, the only person who can give you your identity is you. Do you understand what I'm saying?

You *decide* who you want to be, how you want to be perceived, and what you want others to believe about you. You decide to love yourself for who you are and to carry yourself with confidence.

Let me give you an example. Let's say you're artistic. You love to draw, so you draw when you have downtime in class. You draw on your notebook. You draw in the margins of your papers. People see your drawings, and they say, "Wow. You're talented. You're an artist."

Now, it's nice that other people noticed and reinforced your identity, but really you had already decided you were an artist when you drew that first doodle years ago. You defined yourself, and other people accepted it.

Too many teens spend their time asking, "Who am I?" when that is not the right question. The question is, "Who do I want to be?" Once you decide who you want to be, you just become it, and other people see you as that person.

A comedian might be born with a quirky sense of humor, but that doesn't make him a comedian.

He practices jokes in front of the mirror. He tries them out on friends. He experiments with what makes people laugh. He becomes a comedian in his small circle of influence and other people say, "Gee, you're really funny. You should be a comedian." The truth is, he has already given himself that identity. He chose and claimed that identity, and other people simply reinforced it.

> "The way you treat yourself sets the standard for others."
>
> Sonya Friedman

Don't think you're special?

I can already hear your reply — your excuses. Yeah, yeah, you say. That's fine for someone who has a special talent like art or comedy. I'm just ordinary. I'm not special.

Lean in here closer so I can smack you upside the head.

You're not listening. You *choose* who you want to be.

Take a moment and in your imagination, try on different identities. Imagine yourself as an actress on a stage. Does that feel like something you want? No, okay. Imagine yourself leading a board meeting? No? Imagine yourself cracking open the hood of a car and being able to fix any problem inside. Keep imagining yourself in different roles until one vibrates in you with excitement. Suddenly, there's an image in your mind of you being someone that makes you say, "Yes! I'd do whatever it takes to be that person."

That is how you find your identity. You decide you are that person in the making, and you start doing the things that person would do. Want to be an extreme adventurer like Bear Grylls? You're gonna have to learn to build a shelter and cook over an open fire. You need to be able to read a compass. You take baby steps along the path to becoming. After you've traveled that path for a while, someone will notice (it may take longer than you would like, but eventually someone will notice) and she will say, "Hey, you're really outdoorsy, aren't you? You're so adventurous."

> *"No one can make you feel inferior without your permission."*
>
> *Eleanor Roosevelt*

What does this have to do with confidence?

It's true that some people are born with confidence, while others struggle to obtain it, but if you lack confidence, you're not stuck forever. You claim confidence the same way you claim your identity. You decide to have it, and you practice being confident until it becomes natural. You can become as confident as anyone you know. You simply have to decide you are ready.

Confidence begins with a willingness to love and accept yourself completely.

Stand in front of a mirror. Look into the eyes of the reflection staring back at you, and tell yourself, "I love and accept you completely. I cherish your strengths. I accept all your faults. I will always love you and take care of you. I will stop putting you down and saying mean things to you. I will be your very best friend."

Did you struggle with that? If you struggled with this exercise, if you cannot or will not say those things to yourself, you need to ask yourself why. Why don't you think you are worthy of complete and unconditional love? Who told you that you didn't deserve it? (They lied to you, BTW. You totally deserve it!) Why are you unwilling to be your own best friend and to promise love and loyalty to yourself?

If you are unwilling or unable to give those gifts to yourself, how can you expect others to give the gifts of love and acceptance to you? You know you better than anyone. You know that you are doing your best. You know your own heart. It's time to stop beating yourself up for not being perfect (newsflash—no one is perfect) and accept yourself with grace and honesty. This is the first and most important step to confidence.

Once you decide that you are worth loving unconditionally, you treat yourself with kindness and dignity. You realize that people who put you down or treat you badly are not really your friends. You stop allowing them to heap their garbage on you. You stand up for your friend in the mirror.

EXERCISE:

1. Stand in front of a mirror. Look into the eyes of the reflection staring back at you, and tell yourself, "I love and accept you completely. I cherish your strengths. I accept all your faults. I will always love you and take care of you. I will stop putting you down and saying mean things to you. I will be your very best friend." Write down the feelings and thoughts you have as you do this exercise. Did you struggle? What negative thoughts came up? Write those down and this week work at releasing those negative thoughts.

2. Write down five things you would do if age, time, money, education, and experience were not a factor.

Scan this code to see
the video introduction.

Chapter 5
DON'T OVERLOAD

You wrote down your vision, right? You didn't just skip ahead and keep reading without actually doing the exercise? If you haven't written down your vision, go back and do that now. (Hint: It's at the end of Chapter 3.)

I'll wait.

You're done now? Awesome. Let's move on.

Panic Surrounding College

Nationwide there is a predominant belief among parents, guidance counselors, and high school students that it's harder to get into college these days. This frenzy has fueled a multibillion dollar industry of tutoring, testing, and paranoia.

I went to a parent night at a local high school. The parent night was presented by a husband and wife team whose business was college preparation and test readiness. They suggested teens take the SAT three times so they could get a superscore for their tests. They encouraged Advanced Placement (AP) tests and earning college credits in high school.

Don't get me wrong. I'm not saying those things are inherently bad, but the atmosphere of competition and anxiety surrounding college admissions has reached epic proportions. Whereas AP classes used to be for juniors and seniors, my kids' high school now offers AP classes beginning freshman year. Seventh graders are earning high school credits. The culture of achievement is pushing more, more, more. Take more advanced classes, take more tests, do more test preparation, hire more tutors.

I want you to know the truth about what's driving all this. When the *US News & World Report* began ranking colleges, two of the factors they considered were the test scores of accepted students and the percentage of applicants accepted. The higher the test scores and the lower the acceptance percentage, the higher the school ranked.

Imagine you are a small, liberal arts college in Washington state. You take a class of 500 freshman every year. You receive 1,000 applications for those 500 seats. You have a 50 percent acceptance rate. You decide you want to increase your ranking, so you print out glossy brochures and send them to 50,000 seniors across the U.S., most of whom have never been to Washington state, much less your campus. Suddenly you get 5,000 applications for those 500 spots. Now you can choose kids with higher test scores, and you have a 10 percent acceptance rate. Your ranking soars, but some kid who'd never heard of you a year ago is devastated that he didn't get in.

However, that kid didn't apply to one or two schools, like he might have twenty years ago. No, he applied to ten schools. He can only attend one, but he gets accepted to five.

Here is the truth: While elite schools like Harvard boast a 2-3 percent acceptance rate, there are thousands of schools across the country struggling to fill seats. There are more options than ever before in terms of higher education. Online programs are thriving. Community college are expanding their offerings allowing more students to stay at home or work while attending college. There is no single right way to get an education. There are hundreds of paths that can lead you to a successful life and the career of your dreams.

So, who is profiting most from the college admissions frenzy? In addition to the hundreds of businesses like the one that presented the parent night at our local high school, the biggest winners are colleges themselves and the College Board, which offers AP and the SAT.

How do colleges benefit? Look at the previous example. That small liberal arts college used to get 1,000 applications for 500 seats. Each of those applications came with a $40 application fee. Every year those applications brought in $40,000 to fund their admissions office. Once they begin heavily advertising, they get 5,000 applications times the $40 fee is $200,000. Not a bad payday. Sure, it takes them more manpower to process those applications, but they are still only filling 500 seats.

Now consider the College Board, which is a "non-profit" like the NFL. The College Board administers AP tests in schools around the country.

> "Trying to do it all and expecting it all can be done exactly right is a recipe for disappointment. Perfection is the enemy."
>
> Sheryl Sandberg

Students pay nearly $100 for each AP test. Instead of taking one or two AP classes, many student are taking AP throughout their high school careers. If you have a million students who used to take two tests, that was $200 million dollars. Let's say each of those students now takes six tests, tripling the College Board's payday to $600 million. That's not all. According to the National Center for Educational Statistics 3.5 million high school seniors will graduate this year.[iv] Every senior is encouraged to take the SAT for college admission. The test costs $50 to $75 depending on what extras you select. For the sake of this example, we will use $50. If every graduating senior takes the SAT once, the College Board collects $175 million, but if they can convince seniors they need three tests to superscore, that number suddenly becomes $525 million. Can you see why they want you to think lots of AP tests and three SATs are not only a good idea, but completely necessary to your success?

Guess what? It's simply not true. They are stressing you out to put money in their own pockets.

High school is four short years intended to prepare you for college, trade school, or another career path. Tough academic classes are not the only preparation you need for the next phase of your life.

In an effort to better prepare students for college, high schools are pushing more content and therefore have less time to nurture authentic learning. Colleges complain that freshmen are showing up *less prepared* than ten years ago.

How can this be?

Simple. High school students are stuck in a cycle of study, memorize, test, forget, study, memorize, test, forget. They are learning more and retaining less than ten years ago. Add increases in the number of hours spent on homework and sleep deprivation into the mix, and you get an alarming picture of a "normal" high school experience these days. What is the solution? Don't do it all.

Play to Your Strengths

Business coach Christian Mickelson introduced me to the "cake and cringe" principle.[v] Some classes are interesting and fun to you. Those are your cake classes. Other classes you have to take, even if you hate them. Those are the cringe classes.

For me English and history were cake. Math was okay, but science was a total cringe. I was an honors student who wanted to attend college. I was hoping for an academic scholarship. I was already taking AP English and history, because they were what I liked. Everyone told me I should take AP science classes if I wanted to get into the best college, but I really didn't want to take AP sciences. My senior year I opted out of AP Chemistry and instead took

Advanced Foods.

While they were balancing equations, doing labs I would have hated, and prepping for the AP test, I was baking cookies, making enchiladas, and learning to prepare a perfect omelet. Not only was Advanced Foods fun (we got to eat all of our creations), but I learned real-world skills that I've used hundreds of times. Today I'm a writer. I still enjoy cooking, and I have never regretted opting out of AP Chem. No one has ever asked me to balance an equation in the course of my adult life. Not even once. It is not a real-world skill unless you are a chemist.

Life preparation is more than just grades and tests. When you overload academically, you greatly increase your stress without guaranteeing better long-term results. In fact, you may even sabotage your long-term success. As a future English teacher and writer, I really didn't need AP Chemistry. I still got into college, and I still attended college on an academic scholarship.

Once you graduate from college and get your first job, where you went to school matters far less than what kind of degree you earned. Once you have a few years of job experience, your degree matters less than what you can do and the career experience you have behind you. Most of the people I know do not work in the field in which they got their degrees. They have shifted through several jobs and positions over the course of their careers, and the jobs they now have are the result of their previous job experience, not the degrees they earned years ago.

Playing to your strengths goes against the popular do-it-all mentality, but it will serve you well. I'm not saying you should avoid cringe-worthy classes altogether. Some of them are required for graduation. I am saying it's okay to take easier classes in a cringe-worthy subject and shift the heavier study load to subjects you enjoy.

As you plan out your schedule, leave space for classes you want to take just for fun. Take classes that teach you practical skills that you'll use in day-to-day life. Take classes that will help you manage your money or design a landscape. Take a course in entrepreneurship and learn how to start a business. Take an art or photography class and learn how to see the world the way an artist sees it.

Most of all, try to have fun in your classes. It doesn't have to be four years of endless torture, okay? Put a bright spot in every day. You get to choose the classes you take, so take the ones that serve *you*, not a university to which you haven't even applied. It's your life. It's your education. Make it an experience that serves you and your dreams.

EXERCISE:
1. Look through the required classes for graduation. Decide which classes are your cake classes, and which are your cringe classes. Choose harder coursework in the cake subjects. Then look through the course catalog again. Pick three or four classes that you want to take for fun. Decide where to put these classes in your high school plan. Don't save all the fun for your senior year. Try to take at least one fun class each year of high school.
2. Look over your plans for high school. Do they coincide with your life vision? Are the classes you plan to take the ones that will give you the skills to make your vision a reality?

Chapter 6
SIMPLE SYSTEMS FOR SUCCESS

I taught high school for six years. I taught remedial freshman English, AP Literature and Composition, and most English classes in between. I gave out plenty of A's and B's. I gave out some F's, too. I'm going to tell you some secrets from the other side of the desk. Lean in. This is important.

First, your teachers don't hate you. They don't want you to fail. They don't go home at night and dream up ways to make you miserable. They do go home at night and think about how to better prepare you for the real world. They are often not happy about state and federal requirements that dictate what must be taught and how some things must be graded.

In my classes and in the classes of many of my colleagues, two kinds of students failed — those that didn't show up and those that didn't turn in assignments. I never failed a single student who came to class, did every assignment, and tried to the best of her ability.

Failing because you don't show up is relatively self-explanatory. If you're not there, you can't learn the material. You miss out on in-class assignments, and you fall behind. I never felt bad about failing students with dozens of unexcused absences. They weren't invested in themselves enough to show up, so they deserved to fail.

The second group was far more frustrating to me as a teacher. Some of them were there every single day. I would see them start assignments in class, but those assignments seldom made it into the IN box. The assignments got lost, forgotten, or left at home. These students had the ability to succeed, but they lacked commitment and systems for success.

I don't know about you, but when I was a student, the most stressful times I remember were when I showed up to class, opened my notebook, and realized there was an assignment due and I'd forgotten it, or there was a test, and I'd forgotten to study. I'd sit there in my seat with panic gripping my chest thinking, "I've worked so hard, and now my grade is going to tank. How could I have let this happen?"

Can you relate?

When it comes to academic success, organization is key. You're juggling six classes, activities, chores at home, and a social life. You can't keep it all straight in your head all the time. Things will get forgotten. You drop the ball; your parents tell you you're irresponsible. Maybe you get grounded. You know how this plays out, right?

You can literally organize yourself to A's, and it's not hard to do. You just need a simple system to track tasks. You can use a sheet of notebook paper.

Grab a sheet of lined notebook paper. Divide it into columns and label the columns like this:

Date	Class	Assignment/Test	Text/Supplies	Due Date	Done

Put this tracking sheet in a notebook or folder that you take to every class. Every time your teacher assigns an assignment or announces a test, write it on this tracking sheet. Put any worksheets or packets you need to complete the assignment in the same notebook or folder. Before you leave school at the end of the day, check this task list and make sure you have everything you need to complete your tasks. Check the task list again before you leave for school in the morning to make sure all the assignments are in your notebook, ready to be turned in. This simple system takes about two minutes at the end of every class and another two minutes at the end of school and in the morning before you leave your house. That small investment of time will save you hours of frustration and panic over missed assignments. You'll also be able to stay out of trouble at home. You can add chores and other to-dos to the list so you have all your important things in *one place*.

When you complete the assignment, check it off or write "done" in the Done column. After you turn it in or take the test, cross it off your list. Below is an example.

Date	Class	Assignment/Test	Text/Supplies	Due Date	Done
~~9/14~~	~~History~~	~~Ch 1 Review~~	~~Textbook~~	~~9/15~~	~~Done~~
9/15	English	Character Map	Huck Finn	9/16	

Once you master this simple system, you can expand your organizational system to suit your personality and your classes. The most important thing is that *you have a system* and that it works to effectively track assignments, tasks, and other pressing events.

EXERCISE:
Create a simple system to track tasks by dividing a sheet of notebook paper into six columns. Label the columns: Date, Class, Assignment/Test, Texts/Supplies needed, Due Date, and Done. Place this tracking sheet in a notebook or folder that you take to every class. Begin writing assignments on this sheet and checking it often.

Where does the time go?

Have you ever told your parents (truthfully) that you had too much homework to go somewhere, then you somehow managed to watch three hours of Netflix?

Like goal-setting, somewhere along the way you were probably introduced to the idea of "time management." And, like goal-setting, time management tends to focus on you planning out work instead of fun. Therefore, time management seems like no fun at all, and you probably decided it's not for you.

Instead of managing time, think about being intentional with time. Let's say you get out of school at 3:00 p.m. and you go to bed at 10:00 p.m. You have seven hours between school and bedtime that are yours to fill. Now, I realize you may have obligations that are filling some of those hours. You may play sports, or do a time-consuming activity like drama or dance. You may have a job or major responsibilities with your family.

Still, you only spend about six hours at school every day. You actually have more hours to fill after school than you do during the school day. Did you realize that?

Look back at your vision. This is what you said was your ideal life. In order to make that vision manifest as a reality, you're going to need to take action. Does the way you spend your time reflect that vision?

Let me give you an example. I knew an eleven-year-old boy who used to say he wanted to be a professional football player. He loved football. He could tell you all about various NFL teams. Where was this kid on Saturday mornings? Not out playing football with his friends. No, he was sitting in his basement playing Madden on the Xbox. Do you think he's gonna make it to the NFL? Nope. I don't either. What he said he wanted wasn't actually what he wanted. Guys who love football enough to play as a career want to *play* football, not sit around and pretend to play football. What that boy really wanted was to be rich and famous and have his name on a video game. At eleven, he probably figured professional football was the easiest way to get there. In fact, for someone who doesn't want to get off the couch, it would be nearly impossible for him to manifest that dream.

"Anything worth doing is worth doing poorly until you learn to do it well."

Steve Brown

How you spend your time is an indication of your priorities. That doesn't mean you have to work 24/7 and not relax. On the contrary, you need to relax, which is precisely why I want you to think about how you spend your time.

In high school it seems like there is always more to do. More activities to be involved in, more homework to complete, more time to spend studying, more things you want to do with your friends. At the same time, you are preparing for a life that you're inventing, a life you're envisioning. You want to make sure you meet your immediate needs, but also that you're investing in your future.

They say it takes 10,000 hours to master any skill. There's no shortcut to mastery. If you want to be an artist, you have to put in the time drawing, painting, experimenting, and creating. If you want to be a writer, you have to write. If you want to be a mechanic or an engineer, you have to take things apart, learn how they work, and put them back together.

Remember how I said there were important life skills you can learn outside of school that will prepare you for life? Your vision should drive how you spend your time. Yes, you need to study and you need to finish homework, but the most important part of time management is blocking out time to take care of yourself and pursue your passions.

Get Those Zzzz's

With more homework and more time-demanding activities plus hours on social media, movies, and video games, studies indicate that most teens don't get enough sleep. If you're falling asleep in class (I don't care how boring it is), you're not getting enough sleep. If you need caffeine or lots of sugar to get through the day, you're not getting enough sleep.

Sleep is as vital to your health as food and air. You need sleep. It is essential to your health now and in the future. They say the average teenager needs nine to ten hours of sleep per night. If you're only getting five or six hours of sleep per night, then you sleep in a few extra hours on weekends, you're still not getting all the sleep you need.

Remember it's not just your body that is still growing. Your brain is still developing, too. Sleep provides the much-needed downtime for your brain to fully develop and recover from the rigors of your school day.

Stress and sleep deprivation reduce your ability to reason, to retain what you study, and to recall important information. Basically, sleeping less makes it harder to do well in school and make good decisions. Lack of sleep makes you accident prone, depresses your immune system, and leaves you more susceptible to colds and the flu.[vi]

When it comes to sleep, it's really as simple as, "Pay now or pay later." If you're not willing to take the hours of sleep you need now, you'll most likely end up with an illness, injury, or chronic condition later that will force you to rest.

Our crazy society has prioritized work and studying over sleep. You've heard of college students who crammed all night for exams. That is the *worst* possible way to study. A well-rested brain retains more information. A well-rested brain writes faster, does math faster, and has better higher-level thinking skills than a sleep-deprived brain. That homework assignment that might take 15 minutes when you're wide awake and rested can take 45 minutes to an hour when you're tired.

If you're yawning and having trouble keeping your eyes open while you're doing your homework, stop. Set your alarm for 15 minutes earlier the next morning and go to bed. Don't fall into the trap of scrolling through your phone and checking messages. Put it on "Do Not Disturb" and go to sleep. There is nothing happening on social media that you can't deal with in the morning.

Homework in the morning was one of the single best practices I stumbled upon in college. I was able to spend far less time studying and still get good grades. I have taught it to my kids, and they use it regularly. Without fail, they

> *"A good laugh and a long sleep are the best cures in the doctor's book."*
>
> *Irish Proverb*

get their homework done faster in the morning and they do better on that homework — fewer transposed numbers, dropped decimal points, and misread questions.

I cannot stress enough that sleep should be a priority in your schedule. If you are going to get enough sleep, you have to set a target bedtime. Look, I know you're not six years old anymore, and you pride yourself in not having a set bedtime, but this is part of becoming an adult. You have to be willing to manage your own health instead of having your parents manage it for you. If you're staying up until midnight every night and falling asleep in class, your adulting skills need some improvement.

Even if your homework isn't done, commit to go to sleep at a set time. What time do you need to wake up for school? Count backwards nine hours and that is your target. Try it for a few weeks. You may decide you need less than nine hours of sleep. You may decide you need more. I have one kid who runs perfectly on seven hours of sleep and never feels tired, even when doing endurance sports. I have another kid who needs ten hours of sleep regularly. Only you know how your body feels. Figure out how much sleep you need, and commit to get it. Getting sufficient sleep will allow you to enjoy your waking hours more and to be more effective in everything you do.

Daily Digital Detox

I know you read that subtitle, and you were like, "No! Do whatever you want to me, but DON'T TAKE MY PHONE!"

I get it. Your social life is on your phone. Your phone is your connection to friends, news, information, and entertainment. Whether you're pinning things or scrolling Instagram, your phone is your connection to the outside world.

The problem is that this "connection" keeps you from actually experiencing the world. Instead of having real conversations, you're scrolling and clicking.

This digital world affects your brain. For years therapists and social scientists have been talking about Facebook-induced depression. Too often people compare their imperfect lives to the seemingly perfect lives of others as showcased on Facebook and other platforms.

A recent study indicated that Instagram is the worst app for your mental health. According to the findings, "While the photo-based platform got points for self-expression and self-identity, it was also associated with high levels of anxiety, depression, bullying and FOMO, or the 'fear of missing out.'"[vii]

I know teens who get notifications at all hours of the night. Even with their phones set on vibrate, they are waking up several times a night to read messages and stay in the loop. The constant input overload of our digital world negatively affects your growing brain. It needs time to recover.

Your emotions need downtime, too. While it feels like you can relax and scroll social media, that ritual of relaxation is actually giving your brain hits of serotonin, sapping your motivation, and undermining your overall happiness.

Technology is part of our world. You have grown up with more technology than any generation before you. It's a double-sided sword — a blessing and a curse. You have access to more information, news, ideas, music, and entertainment than any previous generation. A recent article reported that Google CEO Eric Schmidt said that "we create as much information in two days now as we did from the dawn of man through 2003."[viii]

All of that information comes at a price — your mental health. Teens today are more depressed and anxious than their parents and grandparents were. They have more stress.

While you don't have to completely give up technology, you do need to become wiser at using it. Science has proven that the backlight from screens affects sleep patterns, so the best time to detox from technology is at night. Don't fall into the trap of moving from one device to another. It's not a detox if you go from your phone to Netflix. Give yourself technology-free hours.

Set your phone to "Do Not Disturb" at 9:00 p.m. Avoid the temptation to check messages after nine. Tell your friends that you won't respond to their messages if they text you at night. Trust me on this, you will sleep better, have more confidence, and there is nothing happening on social media tonight that you can't deal with in the morning.

EXERCISE:
1. Start by figuring out how many hours you have in a day that you are not in class. Make a list of the most important things you do each week. Make sure to include sleep, homework, and any sports or activities you do regularly. Schedule those essentials into your week.
2. Now block out time to pursue your passions or learn about things in your vision.
3. Set aside some downtime where you can relax and detox from technology. Make downtime an essential part of your busy schedule.
4. Set a target bedtime. Commit to go to bed at that time every day for a week. Record your results.

Chapter 7

THE SECRET TO A
STRESS - FREE LIFE

Stress can have many negative effects on your mental, emotional, and physical health. Below is a list of common effects of stress on your body, your mood, and behavior. Put a mark next to any and all of the effects that you have felt in the past three months.

Common effects of stress on your body:

- Headache or muscle pain
- Fatigue
- Upset stomach
- Trouble sleeping

Common effects of stress on your mood:

- Anxiety
- Restlessness
- Lack of motivation
- Inability to focus
- Feeling overwhelmed
- Irritability or anger
- Sadness or depression

Common effects of stress on your behavior:
- Overeating or undereating
- Being easily angered or frustrated
- Having emotional outbursts
- Drug, alcohol, or tobacco abuse
- Social withdrawal
- Exercising less often

How many symptoms do you have? Three? Six? Ten? More than ten?

Now when you are feeling stressed, you recognize the symptoms. We discussed earlier that school is the most common source of stress among teens, but it's not the only source. Your family relationships, friendships, and work responsibilities can all add to the stress you feel.

What if you could live a completely stress-free life? Wouldn't that feel amazing? Guess what? You can!

Being stress-free feels amazing, and you can have that feeling. Every. Single. Day.

In the next few pages, I'm going to give you five strategies. If you master these strategies, you will be well on your way to being stress-free every day.

The Secret Most Adults Don't Know

Here is the most important thing you need to know about stress. This is a secret. Most adults don't know this, but I'm going to give you the secret now, so your entire life can be stress-free.

Are you ready?

Stress is a state of mind. It is inside your head. It's made of thoughts. Thoughts are so powerful that they can create physical manifestations like sleeplessness, chest pain, weight gain, and hair loss.

You (and only you) control your thoughts, which means that no one can force you to be stressed without your permission. You see, for most people, stress is an automatic response to time constraints. Like, you have a test on Tuesday, and you have fifteen other things to do before that test, so you feel stressed because you don't know if you'll be able to study enough to get a good grade. That is an automatic response for most people, but it doesn't have to be.

> "Most people are about as happy as they make their minds up to be."
>
> Abraham Lincoln

You control your thoughts.

Would you say you're doing the best you can in school right now? Given the amount of time you have to study, the activities you're juggling, and your responsibilities at home, are you doing the best you can? Yes. Of course, you are.

Answer me this. Can you give more than your best?

No. You cannot.

We all hold ourselves to this higher double standard. We do what we can, and then we tell ourselves we should have done more, when in reality, we couldn't do more because there were not enough hours in the day, and you must sleep. Sleep deprivation makes the symptoms of stress worse.

Now, if you're going home and vegging on the couch for three hours every night, then you're stressing about homework, you can obviously change some habits that will give you more study time.

But the fact remains, whether or not you are stressed is your choice because stress is inside your head. Because it's an automatic response, you simply have to learn how to reprogram your thoughts.

I'm going to give you five strategies to manage and reset your stress response. These are the first steps to moving out of stress and anxiety into a state of peace.

1. Deep Breathing

In all of my research on stress and anxiety, this was the number one strategy that came up again and again. It's simple biology. When your body creates a stress response, you breathe shallowly. When you are relaxed, you breathe deeply. Some people (like me) are naturally shallow breathers, and shallow breathers tend to be more stressed and keyed up all the time. By simply teaching yourself to breathe deeply, you can release stress. It's like a system reset for your brain. It's simple, and it works.

Do this: Inhale deeply for three seconds. Breathe all the way into your belly, and let the belly expand as you inhale. Hold for a second or two, then exhale for six seconds. Repeat at least three times.

2. Press Pause on the Panic

All circumstances are neutral. It is our emotional response to those circumstances that decide whether it is positive or negative.

Like me, you might balk at that statement, but understanding the neutrality of circumstances makes you realize just how much power you have to create your own happiness. You can stop a stress response right in its tracks.

Do this: When catastrophe strikes in your life, just pause. Decide not to freak out for three days. If after three days something good has not come of the event, then you can react. In the meantime, say, "I cannot wait to see what amazing things the universe is sending my way thanks to this situation." Something good will come if you are watching for it. The situation may simply resolve itself. Either way, you don't have to be stressed about it in the meantime.

3. Visualize Success

Without realizing it, most of us visualize and attract failure. Think back to the last time you tried something new, or WANTED to try something new, but you chickened out. Most likely, you told yourself all the things that could go wrong. What if this happens? What if that happens?

Instead of expecting the worst and planning for failure, release stress by planning for success. What if the entire Universe was conspiring for your success? What if you could not fail? What would you do then? Visualize yourself succeeding. Focus on that success, and be open to ideas that come to you in the mindset of success.

Do This: Whenever you want to begin a new project, focus on your most desirable end result.

Take three big belly breaths. See yourself getting that result and celebrating. Every time your brain (or someone else) tells you it won't work out, say, "It will work out. I know it will. The entire universe wants me to succeed." Record any ideas that come to you as you visualize success.

4. Smile and Laugh

You know that people smile when they are happy. Did you know that people are happier when they smile? It's true. Studies have proven that when people smiled, they were happier and it lowered their stress. Now, we're not talking about a fake, grit-your-teeth-and-bear-it kind of smile, but a genuine, live-life-to-the-fullest smile.

Do This: Even in your most stressful moments, you can find something to smile about. Maybe it's the sunshine, or the rain, or a flower growing through the sidewalk, or a person you love. Smile because you care. Recognize that love is the driving force behind most of the obligations you fulfill. Smile because you love others and they love you.

5. Choose Happiness

In their book *Stress Free for Good*, Dr. Fred Lusking and Dr. Kenneth Pelletier said, "Most people just aren't happy enough. They aren't getting enough joy out of their lives."[iii]

Happiness can be learned and practiced. It is as simple as shifting your focus from what is wrong with your life to what is awesome. The more you look for things that make you happy in life, the more you will see. Remember that no one can make you happy. You choose it, you find it, and you create it.

Do This: Take time to sit somewhere quiet. Notice how you feel. Does your energy feel light, uplifting and expansive, or do you feel tight, pressed down, and constricted? Focus on things in your life that are good and that bring you joy. Look for wisdom, understanding, and empathy that have come from areas of struggle. Feel gratitude for lessons learned and love received. Whenever things start to go wrong in your circumstances, remember these things that bring you joy.

Understand that you are not obligated to receive anyone else's bad feelings or negative energy. If someone cuts you off in traffic, simply press on the brake and say, "Go ahead. You must be in a hurry."

When someone is rude to you, think, "You must be having a bad day, but I'm going to have a great day, and no one can make it otherwise!"

It takes practice to retrain your thoughts, but you can practice happiness, which is the best long-term stress reliever of all.

EXERCISE:

1. Choose one stress-releasing strategy and practice it several times a day for three days. Notice how you feel before and after using the strategy.

2. Add another strategy each day until you master all five in this chapter.

3. Record your feelings and progress in your journal.

Scan this code to see
the video introduction.

Chapter 8
GET INVOLVED

Have you seen one of those awesome schools that has tons of school spirit and dozens of great activities? Have you also seen a lame school where the bleachers are empty, they host only a couple of dances a year, and even those are boring?

As a former cheer coach and activities advisor at several different schools, I can tell you in one sentence the difference between those two schools. It's really this simple: Kids show up.

It's not the facility, the DJ, the choice of spirit days, or the extravagance of a school activity that determines if it is a success or a total flop. It's the students. Every. Single. Time.

Over the past decade I have watched a sad trend in YA novels, television shows, movies, and music that paints everything school-related as stupid, boring, or shallow.

Think about the YA protagonists in books you've read recently. Most of the heroes are the outcasts, the misfits, the kids who avoid all things school-related. They go to class (because they have to), collect their grades, and nothing more. Prom is beneath them. Cheerleaders are fake, shallow, or mean. Ditto for the jocks, the honor students, you name it. The only "cool kids" are other misfits who abhor school.

How does this influence real schools? Fewer people are in the stands. Fewer tickets are sold to dances. Events get cancelled for lack of interest. Sadly, the same kids who bought the idea that all school activities are lame trade a real social life for fake social media friends and followers.

As an institution the school doesn't need sports or activities. Those things are provided as a service for your social development. If the activities are lame, it's not a reflection of the school or the staff. It's a reflection of you and your peers.

It only takes one involved class to turn the tide in any high school. Often schools look to the seniors to set the tone, but if the senior class has basically checked out of school, there is no reason your freshman class can't set the tone for a completely amazing year. You and your classmates can turn your school around right now. Want to know how? Do three simple things.

Show up.

Get involved.

Have fun.

Most schools offer a wide variety of sports, activities, and clubs. During orientation, you will learn about some of them, but probably not all.

Choose one that sounds fun and join. Show up to every meeting and activity the club plans. Decide right now that you will attend the home football games, dances, and other activities. It only takes a few people having fun to make an activity a success.

> *"The strongest principle of growth lies in human choice."*
>
> *George Eliot*

When I was in high school we had dances after the football games. Sometimes they were packed, and sometimes almost no one showed up. However, we had a co-ed varsity cheer squad of twelve people. Every cheerleader brought someone and danced. The dance floor was never empty. Twenty-four people dancing and having fun was enough. When more people showed up, they joined in.

Consider your circle of friends. Are there five of you? Maybe eight? If you each grabbed one other person to join you, you'd have a dozen friends. You can have fun at a game or dance with a dozen people. You just have to decide to do it.

Most teens don't realize how easy it is to create fun activities. They show up to an event and see a few people milling around. No one is dancing; no one is having fun. From an "entertain me" perspective, they decide to cut and run, as if it were someone else's job to ensure that they had fun.

Only one person is responsible for you having fun at any activity. That person is you.

You can choose to relax and have fun, or you can

choose to be bored, but if someone else is providing the place and music, why not grab your friends and decide to have a good time?

The Power of Purpose

Besides having fun, activities provide you resiliency and social connection. Too many teens feel powerless and frustrated with the world at large. Activities provide a way for you to get involved with causes that matter and are aligned with your vision. In clubs you learn how to serve your fellow students and the community.

Activities also allow you to interact with people outside your normal circle of friends. You'll meet upper classmen who can give you advice and help you feel connected to your school. You'll interact with advisors and administrators. You'll see your school from a different perspective.

All of these things help to shape your high school experience and build your resiliency so when you have tough times (and you will have a few), you will have purpose, connection, and support.

EXERCISE:

1. Look over the sports, clubs, and activities offered by your high school. Choose one or two and join. Decide that you will attend every meeting and event held by your chosen group.

2. Get a calendar of school events. Grab two or three friends and attend several events over the next six weeks. This is a great way to meet new people and start your high school experience off right.

Scan this code to see the video introduction.

Chapter 9
DON'T MAKE FRIENDS. BE A FRIEND

Throughout your adolescence and into adulthood, you will encounter people who are good friends and people who are not. Friendships play an important role in your teen years, probably more so than any other time in your life. Where your world revolved around your family in childhood, in your teens friends become your universe. Teens naturally distance themselves from their parents in an effort to develop independence and personal identity. While families still play a vital role in your life, your friendships have a large and lasting impact on who you become.

The Importance of Good Friends
It's more important than ever that you develop quality friendships that are in alignment with the person you intend to be in the future. The quality of your friendships will affect your happiness because bad friends will drain your energy, stir up drama,

and put you in dangerous situations. Meanwhile, good friendships will help you grow in confidence, allow you to be yourself, have fun, and create happy memories.

Why are good friendships so important in your teen years? For starters, you're developing your own identity, and you will be heavily influenced by who you hang around. You become like the people with whom you spend the most time. This is why it's so important to be choosy in your friends.

A friend is someone with whom you have a bond of mutual affection, exclusive of family relationships, romance, or sexual relationships. To be clear, a friend is someone you can trust, someone who keeps your secrets, someone who does not talk about you behind your back or make you feel insecure. A friend is loyal and defends you when you're not around. A friend helps you become the best person you can be.

Teens often mistakenly believe that any form of acceptance constitutes friendship, which often leads to shallow or damaging friendships. If a certain crowd of girls allows you to sit at their table, but they constantly make you feel insecure or criticize you, that's not friendship. If all you have to do in order to be accepted by the druggies is to start using, that's not friendship either. Friends love and appreciate you for who you are. You have the right to be choosy in your friendships and walk away from friendships that drag you down.

Think about your friends' bad habits for a moment. Do they gossip a lot? Do they swear? Do they smoke or party? Initially, you may not take on these habits, but over time your friends' habits will seem normal to you. You will pick up those habits whether they are good or bad.

Too often teens settle for bad friendships, unaware that they deserve better or because they are unwilling to risk rejection by seeking new friends.

A Politically Incorrect Look at Friendship

While it's not always politically correct to talk about people in terms of social status, let's set those niceties aside for a moment so I can explain a fundamental problem teens have when looking for friends.

Like it or not, there are cliques and groups in high school. Some of these groups are popular or hold a particular social status. In one high school, the athletes may be the popular crowd. In another high school, it's the drama club. In yet another high school, the most popular kids are the high-achievers — the college-bound, 4.0 GPAs. Whatever the case in your school, there are nearly always kids above you in status and kids below you.

The problem for most teens is that they look upward in status when trying to make friends. They unconsciously seek to improve their status through their friendships. This is problematic because it is inherently self-serving. You set out to get someone more popular than you to like you so you can enjoy her status. Essentially, you are using that person, and that is not real friendship.

Consider the case of Isabelle. In the transition to

high school, Isabelle wanted friends. She'd never had a best friend in middle school, and her group of friends had grown apart. She entered high school feeling self-conscious and vulnerable. Her first priority was to make friends. She tried to sit with various groups of girls at lunch, but always felt like an outsider. She joined a club hoping to find friends, but went away disappointed. The girls at

> "I can be changed by what happens to me, but I refuse to be reduced by it."
>
> Maya Angelou

her church were too boring. She wanted cool friends, friends who went out and had fun and laughed themselves silly. By October, Isabelle felt depressed that no one would ever like her. She sat alone in her room instead of going to football games. She trolled social media with envy and felt miserable.

Can you relate to Isabelle's plight?

Here's the problem with Isabelle. She was looking for something friends *would give her* instead of what *she could give* to friends. Isabelle was looking to raise her social status using friendship. She wanted someone else to fix her problems for her. Therefore, she was stuck.

Now consider Jessica's story. Jessica's family moved to a new town two weeks before her sophomore year. The first day of school was a blur of crowded hallways and strangers, but Jessica wasn't trying to fit in. Before starting school she'd decided to do something nice for someone each day. Instead of wondering if people liked her,

Jessica was on the lookout for someone who might need help. At lunch Jessica found a girl sitting alone and asked to join her. She talked with the girl and listened intently. She learned that the school had a service club that worked with local charities. Jessica decided to join the club and went out on several projects. As she worked alongside people from her school, she laughed and talked with them. She felt a sense of accomplishment and camaraderie when they finished a project. It didn't matter that these people weren't exactly like her. For a few hours a week, they had a purpose, and they made a difference in their community. One of the girls — a self-proclaimed loner — invited Jessica to hang out. As they talked Jessica realized this girl was incredibly lonely. Jessica made a point to find the girl every day at school and say hello.

How do you think Jessica's story turned out? Do you think she had friends by the end of first semester? Of course she did.

The difference between Isabelle and Jessica is that Isabelle set out to "make friends." She wanted people to like her. She expected to show up and be welcomed into a friend group. On the other hand, Jessica set out to *be* a friend. She didn't worry about whether or not people liked her. She decided to help people, to be there for someone who was lonely, and to get involved in projects that brought her joy.

When it comes to forming friendships, Jessica's approach is the more successful one. If you are selfishly expecting people to befriend you and make you happy, you've missed the point of what it means to be a real friend. Learning to be a friend may mean taking the time to be kind and talk to people that you ordinarily wouldn't, but isn't that what you want someone to do for you when you're lonely? If you're the girl sitting alone, how do you feel about the person who sits down next to you and takes a real interest in you? Wouldn't you be grateful that someone took the time to notice you?

Gratitude and kindness are excellent starting points for friendship. Of course, not everyone you befriend will become your BFF, but when you stop worrying about *you* and start caring about others, friends are naturally drawn to you. Let me caution you, though; you must be genuine. People can see through fake charity and mock kindness. If your heart's not in it, you should spend some time looking at your heart before you set out to befriend others. Remember that you can decide to be confident. You can decide to love yourself exactly as you are, even if you have no friends. When you are confident, kind, and full of gratitude, you will more easily connect with others and establish lasting, healthy friendships.

EXERCISE:

1. Take a moment and list the qualities you want and need in a good friend. Evaluate your current friendships against this list. Be honest with yourself. Are your friends good for you? Are they helping you reach your dreams or moving you farther away?

2. Focus on one or two qualities you most desire in a friend, such as kindness, honesty, trustworthiness. For the next two weeks, develop those qualities in yourself. Try to get out of your comfort zone and share those good qualities with others.

Scan this code to see
the video introduction.

Chapter 10
STAY OUTTA THE VICTIM TRAP

Thoughts are powerful things. Reinforced thoughts become beliefs. Thoughts and beliefs manifest as tangible results without you even realizing it. You literally create your own reality by what you believe and what you choose as a result of those beliefs. As a child, your reality was based on your parents' beliefs. What they believed, they manifested. That was your reality, so you came to espouse the same beliefs about faith, money, your role in society, and how the world works. As you venture into the world, you encounter other beliefs. Society teaches you its own set of beliefs. The media teaches beliefs that serve its commercial interests. Some of these beliefs you accept (often unconsciously) and some you reject. Eventually, you live by the sum total of beliefs you've collected over your childhood and adolescence. These are the beliefs you take with you into adulthood, and unless you actively work to change them, they are the beliefs that govern the rest of your life.

Many of those beliefs are good and guide you to becoming a healthy, happy person. Some beliefs, however, limit your ability to become everything you are intended to become. These are called self-limiting beliefs. That means you believe something that limits you or holds you back. If you break the belief, you can break through your limitations.

Maybe you've heard people express limiting beliefs like, "I just wasn't born to do great things" or "people like me don't get lucky breaks." These are beliefs that limit their ability to see opportunities that might be right in front of them.

Often people hold onto limiting beliefs that do not serve them because those beliefs are held by other people with whom they associate. Sometimes limiting beliefs are popular and allow you to feel a sense of belonging, even though you trade your joy, abundance, and opportunity for those limiting beliefs.

In American culture there has been a startling and noticeable rise in victimhood beliefs, where people publicize minor slights or "microagressions" as a way of drawing attention to their own suffering and marginalization.[ix] Stuck in their victim mindset, these people try to get others to rally around them in shaming and blaming anyone who mistreats them, no matter how minor the offense. Essentially, this is a culture which seeks popularity by embracing powerlessness, and seeks to blame others for that powerlessness.

In response to this overwhelmingly popular victimhood culture, colleges are creating "safe spaces" and blogs that call out microaggressions while praising those who, instead of directly addressing a problem with the person who offended them, go behind the backs of the offender to gossip on social media about perceived aggression. Blogger Ronald Bailey explained it this way, "the culture of victimization rewards people for taking on a personal identity as one who is damaged, weak, and aggrieved."ˣ

The fact that victimhood is culturally popular is disturbing because it does the opposite of what it claims to do, which is empower victims. Hang onto your hats, kiddos, you're about to be triggered.

Let me make this explicitly clear: You will *never* reach your full potential from a victim mindset. It is *impossible* to hold onto victimhood and become your best self. If you want to become the person who is living your dreams, you have to take full responsibility for your thoughts, words, and results. That means being 100 percent accountable, not passing the blame onto someone else. You may have a bout of bad luck. You may get slighted along the way. No matter who you are, how you look, and what you decide to undertake, you should expect opposition along the way. Victims whine and quit when faced with opposition. Victims go around angry and ready to attack anyone who contradicts their entitlement. None of those traits will lead you to success.

Do you have a Victim Mindset?
Sadly, you've been taught by society to embrace victimhood. Often without realizing it, you take on

a victim mindset. It can be tricky to recognize and weed out victim tendencies that block your progress. So, what is a victim mindset? What does it look like?

A victim mindset:

- Believes she has been wronged
- Feels powerless to change her own circumstances
- Blames others for her own unhappiness
- Believes she has no control over life
- Assumes the worst about people and situations
- Is defensive
- Puts herself down
- Wants sympathy
- Refuses to try to improve
- Is passive aggressive

Remember how I told you that thoughts are so powerful that they actually attract results into your life. The same is true of negative thoughts as much as positive thoughts. When you try to set a new goal and move forward, the victim mindset basically creates a brick wall through which you cannot pass. The victim mindset is the flow-stopper in attracting what you *really* want out of life.

Now, you may have read over that list and said, "I'm not like that. That's not describing me at all." Sometimes the victim mentality tricks you into believing it's everyone else's problem, but not yours. So, be honest with yourself.

1. When you chat with your friends, do you often talk about how hard your life is?
2. Do you ever tell yourself no one

appreciates you or understands you?

3. Do you feel that life is unfair and that you never get what you deserve?

4. Do you secretly wish bad things would happen to happy and successful people to take them down a notch?

5. Do you refuse to set goals because you don't think you can reach them?

6. Do you wish that someone would come along and save you from your problems?

7. When change comes into your life, do you automatically imagine worst-case scenarios of what it will mean for you?

8. Do you exaggerate your feelings or problems to get attention or sympathy?

If you answered yes to any of these questions, or if they gave you a pang of guilt, your mindset could use some work.

Mastering the victim mindset is not just about looking on the bright side or being grateful for what you have, although a positive attitude and gratitude are both valuable traits that will bring you better long-term results. If your thoughts, words, and beliefs are painting you as victim, they will keep you stuck in unhappy and painful places until you decide victimhood no longer serves you.

Losing a victim mindset goes much deeper than simply being cheerful. It means you are willing to take complete responsibility for every aspect of your life, including your thoughts, words, beliefs, and actions. It means you're ready to stop blaming and pointing fingers. It means that when you don't like some aspect of your life, you decide to change it even if it takes time, effort, and patience.

Accept that there will be haters in your life no matter what. Accept that some people will never get on board with your dreams. Accept that no matter what anyone else says or does, *you and only you determine the course of your life*. When you decide to be 100 percent accountable for your own dreams, when you decide that nothing will stop you from becoming who you dream of becoming, you will overcome victimhood and be on your way to success.

<u>EXERCISE:</u>
1. Review the victim mindset. Do you exhibit any of the victim tendencies? Be honest with yourself. Write down which thoughts and beliefs you struggle with. List the tendencies and describe how you will be accountable for them instead of blaming someone or something.
2. Look at your list of victimhood thoughts. Reword them into empowered thoughts. For example, if you often think, "No one appreciates me," reword that as an empowered statement like, "I am valuable, unique, and I am appreciated by myself and others." Read this empowered statement every morning and every night for two weeks. Then record how you feel.

Scan this code to see
the video introduction.

Chapter 11

SET PERSONAL BOUNDARIES AND STICK TO THEM

One of my intentions in writing this book is to educate you on topics about which most adults are remaining silent. I believe that knowledge is power, so I'm not going to shy away from some of the tough things you face every day.

Let's start with some questions:

- Have you or one of your friends ever been asked to send nude photos to a guy?
- Have you or one of your friends ever been sent unsolicited pornographic photos?
- Do you know of others who send nude photos to guys?
- Have you ever been expected to participate in a sexual encounter without any existing relationship or emotional intimacy?

- Have you ever been offered alcohol at a party?

Before we start talking about personal boundaries, I want you to understand why you need them. You're growing up in a culture that is saturated with violent, degrading pornography. More than any other influence in society, pornography demeans women. Pornography glorifies the rape and abuse of women. At a time when women's rights and equality are commonplace, pornography is the disease that undermines our forward progress because it teaches men and boys that women are disposable objects that enjoy being beat up, assaulted, used, and left alone.

Many adults embrace pornography as a safe alternative to teen sexual activity, but that is simply not true. Pornography is linked to the normalization of sexual violence, skyrocketing incidents of child sexual abuse, sex trafficking, depression, and anxiety.[xi]

As young women, you and your friends suffer the most in this new culture of sex and violence.

Teen girls are looking for love and romance. I get it. You want to be cherished and understood. Meanwhile, boys of the porn-drenched culture are looking for emotionless, zero-commitment hook-ups, hence the request for nude photos. If you refuse, he immediately loses interest and moves on.

Increasingly teens are feeling pressure to participate in hook-ups. Hook-ups are uncommitted sexual encounters. "Hook-up activities may include a wide range of sexual behaviors, such as kissing, oral sex, and penetrative intercourse. However, these encounters often transpire without any promise of—or desire for—a more traditional romantic relationship."[xii]

Movies, television, and music videos increasingly portray hook-ups as the most desirable sexual encounters—the pleasure of sex without the messy strings attached. However, in real life, the hook-up culture is taking a toll on the mental and emotional health of teens and young adults, particularly girls.

With most boys encountering pornography for the first time in early elementary school, is it any wonder that many girls reported that their first sexual encounter was not a kiss but oral sex, an act girls were expected to perform on boys whether the girls enjoyed it or not? In fact, for most girls their own sexual pleasure is not even part of the equation. They participate in sex, not because it feels good, but because it makes boys happy.

Girls, this is a problem.

Let me make this explicitly clear. You do not owe any guy sex, even if you are in a relationship, even if he says he loves you, even if he says he needs it. You are not obligated to provide sex to anyone. Any guy who demands nude photos or sexual acts before he will commit to you is a user and a player. He will never respect you, and he will never treat you as an equal.

Many girls feel pressured into sexual relationships. Hooking up allows boys to take sex from girls without any commitment. It further perpetuates the idea that women are objects to be used, not people to be loved. By hooking up, girls objectify themselves as one-dimensional sexual beings.[xiii] Their sexuality becomes the measure of their worth, when they have so much more to offer the world than sex. Add alcohol and social media into the mix, and you have a recipe for disaster.

The hook-up culture does not empower girls. It does not serve girls' best interests. Girls are being told that sex is liberating and fun, yet it's leaving them feeling empty and worthless. One in four sexually active girls reports feeling depressed all, most, or a lot of the time.[xiv] Suicide attempts among sexually active girls are double that of non-active girls.

Meanwhile over 60 percent of sexually inactive girls say they are rarely or never depressed. Connect the dots, and you see a startlingly different picture than the media wants you to believe.

Girls who wait to have sex have higher self-esteem, less depression, less anxiety, and lower incidents of suicide.

Multiple sexual encounters with no commitment leave girls feeling jaded. Among teens, we are seeing increasing incidents of not only depression and anxiety, but cutting, burning, and other means of self-harm. You probably know someone who cuts, or you may have done it yourself.

The self-loathing and emptiness girls feel that

leads them to cut or burn themselves is a direct result of the sexual culture that tells them the most important aspiration is to be thin, hot, and sexy. Then when girls play the role of thin, hot, and sexy, they get used and are left feeling hollow. By nature teen girls want to fall in love and feel the excitement of a budding romance, but the hook-up culture sabotages them.

What No One is Telling You About Alcohol
In 2013, half a dozen high-profile rape cases hit the news. Audrie Potts, age 15, killed herself after being raped and cyber-bullied about the attack. Rehtaeh Parsons, a teenage girl from Nova Scotia, also committed suicide after being raped, photographed, and bullied about the attack. Two football players were found guilty of rape in Steubenville, Ohio, and two others traded graphic testimony to escape prosecution. A woman at the Naval Academy accused three Midshipmen of raping her at a party. In Maryville, Missouri, two girls, aged 13 and 14, were raped by older boys; then the community ran one girl's family out of town.

Cases like these are an all-too-familiar headline in our news feeds. A lot has been said, tweeted, blogged and commented about all of them. The cases nearly all involve some sort of victim-blaming. They nearly all involve young (mostly teenage) men. Many involve social media, smartphones, photos, and video. Every single one of the cases involved alcohol.

On one side people condemn the boys, saying

our society is not teaching men to respect women. On the other side, people are condemning the girls. Still others are condemning the bystanders who watched these acts happen, recorded them, and shared them. Then there are the bullies, the "friends" who took to social media to harass the victims until they couldn't take it anymore. Yet no one in the media, on blogs, or on social media was talking about the elephant in the room—alcohol.

A 2009 study looked at drinking as a risk factor for rape.[xv] The findings were startling—horrifying, frankly. Drinking did not double the risk of being raped. Drinking did not triple the risk of being raped. Drinking did not 10x a woman's chances of being raped.

No, intoxication increased the risk of rape *nineteen* times. That is 1900 percent!

Imagine you've just turned 16, and your parents said they'd buy you a brand new car. You can pick out any car you want. You go to the car dealership and you find two awesome cars that you love. On the outside they look nearly identical. They are the same price. However, when you talk to the salesman, he informs you that one of the cars has no safety features whatsoever. If you get into an accident, it is 19 times more likely to kill you.

Would you buy that car?

No. I wouldn't either. Yet, girls all over the country go to parties and drink without understanding the risk. If they drink, they are 19 times more likely to be raped.

The study also showed that drinking by the

perpetrator did not play a factor. Do you understand what I'm saying? If a girl is intoxicated, guys take that as a green light to have sex with her, whether she wants it or not. It doesn't matter if the guy is drunk or sober. What mattered was that the *woman* was intoxicated. Every one of the cases I cited above demonstrates the reality of the study's findings.

Girls, you need to understand this danger. I know you think you can go to a party, drink, dance, and laugh with your friends. That is not the reality. The reality is much darker. It is much more dangerous. No one has been telling teen girls about this risk. If you drink, there is a *very high chance* that you could be sexually assaulted.

When I explain this to girls, some of them say, "We always go in groups. We go with people who will keep us safe." Yet, every day girls are assaulted by the very "friends" who said they would get them home safely. It happens again and again. Going in groups won't protect you.

If you want to reduce your risk of sexual assault, the single most important thing you can do is abstain from alcohol. It's that simple.

Some of you reading this know what I'm saying is true because it happened to you. To be clear, if you were raped, you were the victim of a crime whether you were drunk or not. You weren't "asking for it," and you should seek help. You may be asking, "Why didn't someone warn me?"

Honestly, I don't know, but I'm telling every

girl I can, and I hope you will, too.

Thriving in this Dangerous Culture

So, how does a girl not only survive but thrive in this porn-drenched, intoxicated, hook-up culture? How does a girl find authentic relationships and yes, love, in a use-and-be-used society?

She sets personal boundaries.

Most people never think about what they want and how they will act until they are faced with a choice. Because they have to make split-second decisions under peer pressure, they go along with the crowd and end up in high-risk situations. "Going with the flow" will not serve you well in high school. You have to be intentional about your choices in order to get what you want most.

The way you thrive in high school (and in life) is to decide right now who you are, how you will act, and what you will accept from others. You set personal boundaries and stick to them.

We've already talked about the dangers of alcohol, but it's up to you to decide. Will you drink? Will you attend parties where alcohol is being served? What about other substances? How will you react when (and, I do mean when, not if) you are offered marijuana, cocaine, meth, and other substances? Decide where you will draw the line in the sand and say, "I will never do that."

Now consider your boundaries in romantic relationships. It's natural to want to be loved, but if you have to sell your soul (or your body) for it, it's not worth it. Too many girls compromise what they want just to have a boyfriend. They somehow think that being in a relationship will solve all their problems. What many girls don't realize is that bad relationships are worse than being alone. If you cannot love and respect yourself without a boyfriend, you will end up in unhealthy relationships that further tear you down instead of building you up. High school is not the world. Most people don't find the love of their lives in high school.

Don't hang your hopes and happiness on the people you know right now. Instead, begin thinking of the qualities you want in a life-long partner. Maybe you want someone who understands your love of music like this guy, but who has an off-hand sense of humor like that guy.

Keep your expectations in check. People don't break your heart; they break your expectations. In high school most relationships don't last forever. The key is understanding how each relationship serves you long term. If this doesn't last, will I be a better person for having been in this relationship, or will it leave me scarred and jaded? Your goal in high school is to have the kind of relationships that will leave you a better person, more understanding, more empathetic, a better communicator. Steer away from any relationship that requires you to sacrifice your better judgement, your values, or your safety.

Think of physical relationships on a range from holding hands to kissing to sexual intercourse. What are you comfortable with and when? What is okay in the early stages of a relationship? What is not okay with you? Under what circumstances do you want to have sexual intercourse and in what kind of relationship? What's non-negotiable for you? Write it down, so if anyone crosses that line, you know it's time to walk away. Non-negotiables might include cheating, lying, any kind of physical or emotional abuse. Decide right now what you will not tolerate in a relationship — not even once, no matter how sorry he claims to be.

When you decide what you want, what you will do, and what you won't do, it's easier to walk away from things that don't serve your best interest because you will know that what you are doing is right for you. Personal boundaries empower you because they keep you in control of your own life. Instead of giving your power away to others, you retain that power. You set your own course. Personal boundaries allow you to live proactively instead of reactively. When you live with intention, you live from a place of confidence and empowerment.

EXERCISE:
Set your personal boundaries right now. Write down your boundaries in terms of physical relationships, drugs, and alcohol. What things are non-negotiable for you? Without the influence of your friends, decide what feels right for you. Commit to keep your personal boundaries and help others to do the same.

Scan this code to see
the video introduction.

Chapter 12
ASSESS AND REDIRECT

Life coach Mary Morrissey says there is no such thing as failure, only feedback.[xvi] Whenever things aren't going the way you hoped they would, it may be the Universe telling you that your methods aren't working. It's time to try a new approach.

As human beings, we are creatures of habit, but your current knowledge and habits can only take you so far. Eventually you will come up against limiting beliefs that stop your progress and keep you stuck.

If you keep doing the same things, you will get the same results. Working harder isn't always the answer to changing your life. Often real change means changing your approach—coming at a problem from a different direction.

In this book you have learned important skills for creating vision, stepping into your most confident self, and putting yourself in a position to succeed at your dreams. However, the path to success at anything is rarely straight. Most people take long, uphill detours. They have to fight through disappointments and learn to keep going.

The beauty of life is that you are never really stuck. At any point you can decide that you don't like where you are, and you can choose a different path. The single most important gift you have in life is the freedom of choice. With that freedom you can assess your progress and redirect your efforts.

Stop, Look, and Feel

Have you ever felt like you were caught on a hamster wheel of school, sports, activities, and obligations? Have you ever felt like you could barely keep up, and you were just going through the motions? It's times like that when you need to stop and take a good, hard look at what is really going on in your life. What things are giving you joy, and what things are not? What is moving you closer to your goals, and what is not? Who are the people who are helping you cope, energizing your heart, and making you happy? Who are the people who are draining your energy and bringing you down? Look around your life and allow yourself to be honest about your feelings. What feels right and amazing? What doesn't?

Take the time to assess your happiness and your progress. Breaks from school are an excellent time to assess and redirect. Redirect your energy if you aren't getting to where you want to be. Assess how your methods are working. Are your study habits getting you the grades you want? Do you need to learn new skills? Are your relationships healthy?

Are there friendships that you need to let go, or at least give yourself some distance?

Once you determine where you are in relation to your goals, choose small steps to redirect your energy toward the things you want most.

As you assess and redirect, pay particular attention to your relationship with your family and long-term friends.

Often as teens try on new identities, they rebel against their "old" identities and their families' values. Then they say, "This is the new me, and I'm happy," but their results speak otherwise. They manifest broken relationships, dangerous situations, drug and alcohol use to numb their feelings, and they make little progress toward meaningful goals.

"Happiness cannot be traveled to, owned, earned, worn, or consumed. Happiness is the spiritual experience of living every minute with love, grace, and gratitude."

Denis Waitley

Your authentic identity will rarely require rebellion. It's the very best of all the qualities in you. Developing your authentic self brings light, upward flowing energy into your life. This is the energy of compassion, understanding, and forgiveness. It mends relationships instead of breaking them. It flows with joy that doesn't need numbing.

So, when you stop and assess your life, be brutally honest with yourself. When you look in the mirror, do you see your *very best self* looking back at you? If not, be honest with yourself about why.

With this book you have the tools to allow your very best self to emerge. Don't worry if it takes time and practice. We are all on this journey together. You never walk alone.

Most importantly, remember that you are unique. You are priceless, and you are divine. You have an individual life mission that no one else can fulfill. Whenever you doubt yourself or wonder if you're good enough, please know that you are more than enough. You are absolutely amazing.

You will do great things.

Scan this code for
Michelle's final thoughts
and a special invitation.

REFERENCES

i. Abeles, Vicki. *Beyond Measure: Rescuing an Overscheduled, Overtested, Underestimated Generation*, 2015.

ii. Mayo Clinic Staff. *Healthy Lifestyle, Stress Management, "Chronic Stress Puts Your Health at Risk,"* 2017. http://www.mayoclinic.org/healthy-lifestyle/stress-management/in-depth/stress/art-20046037

iii. Luskin, Dr. Fred, and Dr. Kenneth P. Pelleteir, *Stress Free for Good*, 2005, Harper Collins, New York, New York. 223 pages. Page 45.

iv. Institute of Education Sciences – National Center for Education Statistics, "Back to School Statistics," 2017, https://nces.ed.gov/fastfacts/display.asp?id=372

v. Mickelsen, Christian, *Abundance Unleashed, Open Yourself to More Money, Love, Health, and Happiness Now*, Hay House, Inc., 2017.

vi. http://www.healthline.com/health/sleep-deprivation/effects-on-body

vii. McMillan, Amanda. "Why Instagram is the Worst Social Media for Mental Health." Time. May 25, 2017. http://time.com/4793331/instagram-social-media-mental-health/

viii. Seigler, M.G. "Eric Schmidt: Every 2 Days We Create As Much Information As We Did Up To 2003." TechCrunch. August 4, 2010. https://techcrunch.com/2010/08/04/schmidt-data/

ix. http://reason.com/blog/2015/09/08/the-rise-of-the-culture-of-victimhood-ex

x. Bailey, Ronald. "The Rise of the Culture of Victimhood Explained," reason.com. September 8, 2015.

xi. Jensen, Kristen A. *Protect Young Minds*. 2017. www.protectyoungminds.org

xii. Garcia, Justin R., Chris Reiber, Sean G. Massey, and Ann M. Merriwether. "Sexual Hookup Culture: A Review." *Review of General Psychology*. 2012, American Psychological Association, Vol. 16, No. 2, 161–176

xiii. Henshaw, Stephen and Rachel Kranz. *The Triple Bind, Saving Our Teenage Girls from Today's Pressures*, Ballatine Books, 2009.

xiv. Shapiro, Ben. *Porn Generation: How Social Liberalism is Corrupting Our Future*. Regnery Publishing, 2005.

xv. Testa, Maria and Jennifer A. Livingston, "Alcohol Consumption and Women's Vulnerability to Sexual Victimization: Can Reducing Women's Drinking Prevent Rape?" *Subst Use Misuse*. National Institute of Public Health, Author Manuscript, November 29, 2009.

xvi. Morrissey, Mary. "Dreambuilder," LifeSOULutions That Work. 2017.

GIRLS CHANGE THE WORLD

We are dreamers. We are leaders.
We are visionaries. We are goal-setters.
We are change-makers.

We are a powerful force for good in the
world.

WE ARE GIRLS.
GIRLS CHANGE THE WORLD,

Join us!

Make a difference. Start a movement.
Change the world.

WE WILL DO IT TOGETHER.

https://girls-change-the-world.mn.co